The KidHaven Science Library

The Earth

by Peggy J. Parks

KIDHAVEN PRESS
An imprint of Thomson Gale, a part of The Thomson Corporation

THOMSON

GALE

Detroit • New York • San Francisco • New Haven, Conn. • Waterville, Maine • London

© 2008 Thomson Gale, a part of The Thomson Corporation.

Thomson and Star Logo are trademarks and Gale and KidHaven Press are registered trademarks used herein under license.

For more information, contact
KidHaven Press
27500 Drake Rd.
Farmington Hills, MI 48331-3535
Or you can visit our Internet site at http://www.gale.com

LIBRARY OF CONGRESS CATALOGING-IN-PUBLICATION DATA

Parks, Peggy J., 1951-
   The Earth / by Peggy Parks.
     p. cm. — (Kidhaven science library)
   Includes bibliographical references and index.
   ISBN 978-0-7377-3776-9 (hardcover)
   1. Earth—Juvenile literature. 2. Geology—Juvenile literature. 3. Geologists—Juvenile literature. I. Title.
   QB631.4.P38 2008
   525—dc22
                                              2007022031

ISBN-10: 0-7377-3776-X
Printed in the United States of America

Contents

Chapter 1

An Ancient Planet

One of the greatest mysteries of science is how Earth came to be. No one knows for sure how it formed, or exactly how old it is. But after centuries of study, scientists have developed theories. Most of them say that Earth began about 4.6 billion years ago. They believe the Sun formed first, in the center of a huge cloud of hot gas and dust known as a **nebula.**

Over a very long time, the nebula began to collapse. As it grew smaller, it flattened into a disk. It began spinning faster and faster around the newborn Sun. Gas and dust particles left over from the Sun's formation collided and stuck together. This formed clumps of matter called planetesimals. Gravity drew the planetesimals together. They joined to form larger bodies that eventually became Earth and the other planets.

Growth and Change

For hundreds of millions of years, Earth was a violent, hostile place. Meteors, asteroids, and other space debris constantly smashed into the planet. These collisions generated an enormous amount of heat. They turned Earth into a mass of fiery explosions, thick smoke, and hissing steam. There was no solid surface, because rocks melted in the high temperatures.

Metallic rocks, composed mostly of iron, were the heaviest rocks. As they melted, these **molten** rocks sank deep within Earth to form its **core**. Lighter molten rocks formed the **mantle**, or the layer surrounding the core. After the planet began

The Sun was formed by a nebula, possibly one like the Crab Nebula (pictured).

to cool, some of the molten rock floated to the surface and hardened. It formed Earth's rigid, rocky top layer known as the **crust**.

Earth from the Inside Out

Scientists compare Earth's layered structure to a boiled egg. The yolk, or core, is divided into two parts: an inner core and an outer core. The inner core is a ball of solid iron about 775 miles (1,250km) thick. It is extremely hot—as much as 12,000°F (6,600°C). The outer core is a sea of molten iron about 1,350 miles (2,200km) thick. It is also very hot. Scientists say that as Earth rotates, the outer

The Earth has a layered structure, composed of the inner core, outer core, mantle, and crust.

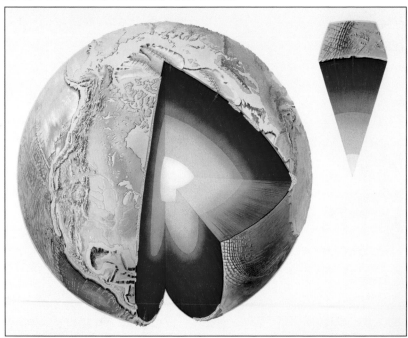

core constantly spins. This creates a magnetic field that keeps the planet from flying out of orbit and hurling off into space.

The mantle is about 1,800 miles (2,900km) thick. It surrounds the outer core and is the largest of Earth's layers. The mantle makes up nearly 80 percent of the planet's total volume. The lower part of the mantle is called the asthenosphere. It is made of hot, semisolid material. The asthenosphere is soft and pliable, much like Silly Putty. In contrast, the upper mantle is cooler and more rigid. Together with the crust, it forms a layer of rock called the lithosphere.

The crust in the top part of the lithosphere is hard and brittle. Its thickness varies based on whether it is beneath the continents or the oceans. The **continental** crust is made of lighter rock but is much thicker than the **oceanic** crust. Earth's mountains rest on crust that is as much as 62 miles (100km) thick. The rest of the continental crust is from 20 to 25 miles (32 to 40km) thick. Oceanic crust is made of heavier rock, but it averages only about 3 miles (5km) thick.

The Blue Planet

The greatest amount of Earth's crust is oceanic. That is because the vast oceans cover more than 70 percent of the planet's surface. There are five major oceans: the Pacific, Atlantic, Indian, Antarctic, and

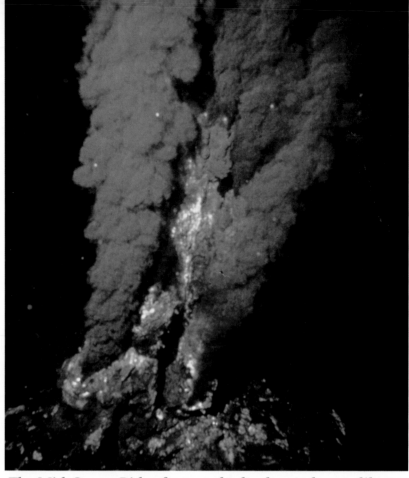

The Mid-Ocean Ridge features hydrothermal vents like this one near California.

Arctic, as well as several dozen smaller seas. Scientists believe that these bodies of water were created when Earth first began to cool. Science writer Lynn Rosentrater explains: "Millions of years ago there were no oceans on the planet. The surface of the Earth was so hot that water simply boiled away. But volcanoes poured huge amounts of steam into the atmosphere and as the Earth cooled down the steam turned to water vapor that condensed as droplets and began to fall as rain. This downpour lasted for many thousands of years filling great hollows in the land and thus forming the world's first seas."[1]

The oceans hold many mysteries for scientists. Because these bodies of water are so enormous, only a small fraction of their depths has been explored. But research has shown that ocean floor landscapes are just as varied as those on the continents. There are vast underwater mountain ranges, such as the Mid-Ocean Ridge. It zigzags its way between the continents and through all the major oceans. The Mid-Ocean Ridge is almost 40,000 miles (64,000km) long—four times longer than the Andes, Rockies, and Himalayan mountain ranges put together.

The deepest point on Earth, the Mariana Trench, appears here as a dark blue crescent on the upper left.

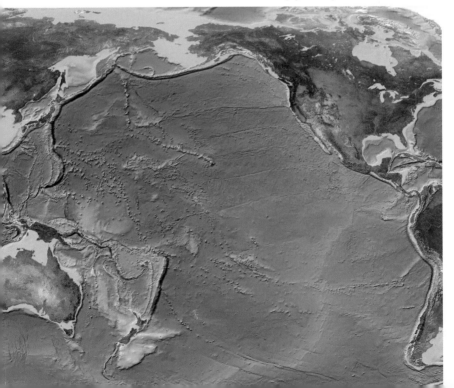

The ocean floor is also carved by huge trenches. The U.S. Geological Association (USGS) describes what they are like: "If by magic we could pull a plug and drain the Pacific Ocean, we would see a most amazing sight—a number of long narrow, curving trenches thousands of kilometers long and 8 to 10km deep cutting into the ocean floor."[2] The deepest point on Earth is the Mariana Trench, which is located in the western Pacific. It is an amazing 36,198 feet (11,033 m) deep. The tallest building in the world is the Taipei 101 in Taiwan. If twenty of these buildings were stacked on top of each other in the Mariana Trench, there would still be nearly a half-mile (.80k) of water covering them!

Earth's Blanket

Unlike the oceans and land, Earth's atmosphere is invisible. It is also quite thin compared to the thickness of Earth. Scientists liken the atmosphere to an orange rind, with Earth as the orange. Yet as thin as the atmosphere is, it is essential for life. It surrounds the planet like a protective blanket. It makes the air fit for humans and other living things to breathe. It also acts as a natural thermostat. The atmosphere holds just the right amount of the Sun's energy to keep Earth from becoming too hot or too cold. In contrast, the Moon has no atmosphere. This creates enormous swings in temperature on the Moon. During the day, it can get as hot as 260°F

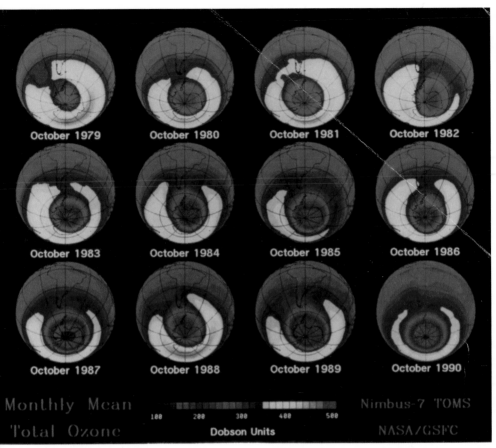

October 1979	October 1980	October 1981	October 1982
October 1983	October 1984	October 1985	October 1986
October 1987	October 1988	October 1989	October 1990

Monthly Mean Total Ozone

100   200   300   400   500
Dobson Units

Nimbus-7 TOMS
NASA/GSFC

Scientists have charted ozone layer depletion from 1979 to 1990.

(127°C). At night, temperatures plummet to -280°F (-173°C).

Earth's atmosphere has four layers. Closest to the surface is the troposphere, which holds about 95 percent of the air. There, weather patterns and clouds form. Above that is the stratosphere. It contains the protective **ozone layer** that screens out the Sun's harmful ultraviolet rays. The ionosphere is where meteors often burn up before they can reach Earth. It is also the atmospheric layer that makes radio communication possible. Without it, radio waves would simply shoot off into space. The top atmospheric layer is the exosphere. It stretches to more than 600 miles (965k) above Earth's surface, where it blends into outer space.

Earth is a fascinating planet whose past is shrouded in mystery. As scientists continue to study it, they become more confident in their theories. But the truth about Earth and how it came to be may never really be known.

Chapter 2

Earth on the Move

About 250 million years ago, Earth's continents looked nothing like they do today. Most scientists believe they were not separate continents at all. Instead, they were part of one enormous mass of land, or supercontinent, that was surrounded by a vast ocean. Scientist Kirk Maasch explains: "You could basically walk from South America into Africa, or from Africa into Australia. If you want to try that today, you'd better buy some fins—you're in for the swim of a lifetime."[3]

Drifting Land

Scientists were curious about the continents as early as the 1500s. Maps showed that Africa and South America looked like pieces of a puzzle that were made to fit together. But it was not until the early 1900s that the idea of moving continents became a serious scientific issue.

A German meteorologist named Alfred Wegener devoted his career to studying the continents. He, too, was curious about their shapes. He was also

Earth's continents were once joined in a supercontinent known as Pangaea, shown in this computer image.

fascinated by other discoveries. Identical plant and animal fossils had been found on the coastlines of Africa and South America—even though the continents were separated by the Atlantic Ocean. Wegener reasoned that the organisms could never have swum or been transported across such a vast body of water. Also, coal deposits had been discovered on Antarctica. Since they were ancient remnants of lush tropical forests, Wegener wondered, how did they arrive in such a frozen, barren land? And why were signs of ancient glaciers found in the sweltering hot Sahara Desert? Wegener believed there was only one explanation for these strange occurrences: The continents were most certainly joined at one time. For some unknown reason, they had split apart and then drifted to new locations. He called his theory **continental drift**. He also gave the former supercontinent a name: Pangaea, which means "all lands."

Wegener first made his findings public in 1915. He wrote: "It is just as if we were to refit the torn pieces of a newspaper by matching their edges and then check whether the lines of print ran smoothly across. If they do, there is nothing left but to conclude that the pieces were in fact joined in this way."[4] As confident as he was in his theory, however, he could not convince his fellow scientists. They criticized and ridiculed him. Even if there was once a supercontinent, they asked, what forces could possibly be strong enough to break it apart and move huge masses of land? Wegener could not answer them. He was sure the continents had drifted, but he had no idea why or how.

A Mystery Solved

More than twenty years after Wegener's death, scientific findings proved him right. **Geologists** studying the ocean floor discovered huge bands of ridges. They could see that new oceanic crust was forming

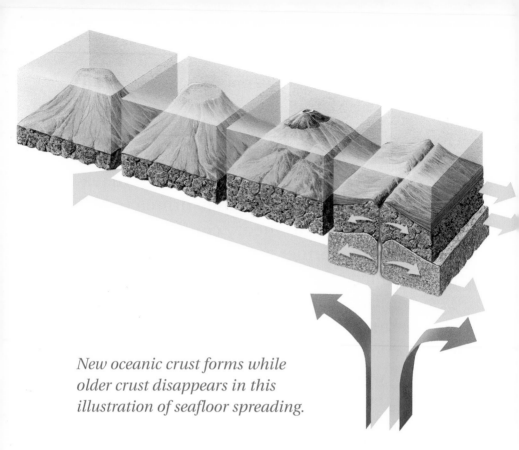

New oceanic crust forms while older crust disappears in this illustration of seafloor spreading.

near the ridges. In other areas of the ocean, older crust was disappearing.

The geologists were amazed by this phenomenon, which they called seafloor spreading. It meant that not only had Earth shifted in the past, it was still moving. Over millions of years, this movement had caused vast changes in the oceanic crust. The USGS explains: "Seafloor spreading over the past 100 to 200 million years has caused the Atlantic Ocean to grow from a tiny inlet of water between the continents of Europe, Africa, and the Americas into the vast ocean that exists today."[5]

As the geologists continued their research, they found significant changes in continental crust, too.

Their findings led to a new scientific theory known as plate tectonics. Finally there was an explanation for the movement of continents.

The Earth on Plates

According to plate tectonics, Earth's crust is divided into gigantic slabs of rock known as plates. The plates are never still. Much like rafts floating on water, they float on the asthenosphere. Science writer Joseph Verrengia explains: "The crust is not solid and unbroken like the coating on a gumball. Rather, it is fractured into more than a dozen overlapping, rigid plates of rocky armor. The plates move . . . as they slide atop the hotter layer below."[6] Earth's plates move very slowly, about 2.5 inches (6.4cm) per year. That is only about twice as fast as fingernails grow. Yet over millions of years, the plate movement has greatly altered the planet.

At their boundaries plates can behave in different ways. They may gently slide past each other. They may continuously rub and grind against each other. They may pull apart, or even smash

The boundaries of Earth's tectonic plates can be seen in this illustration.

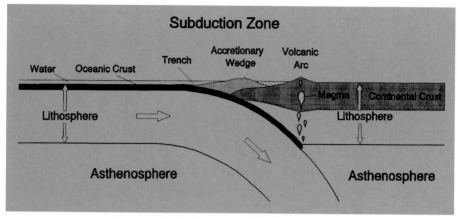

At a subduction zone, heavy oceanic plates are shoved under lighter continental plates.

into each other. When oceanic and continental plates collide, the heavy oceanic plate is shoved under the lighter plate. This is known as **subduction**, and it is how ocean trenches are created. Sometimes subduction causes oceanic plates to be swallowed up by continental plates. That is happening today off the coast of Oregon. A small plate known as Juan de Fuca is slowly sinking beneath the massive North American plate. According to the USGS, the smaller plate will continue to sink until it disappears.

Most of the boundaries between plates are not visible, because they are hidden beneath the oceans. But sometimes boundaries between continental plates can be seen because of **faults**. These are cracks in the crust caused by plate movement miles below the surface. When plates constantly grind or crunch together, it puts great stress on the crust. Because it is fragile, the crust can break like the shell of an egg. Faults may be single fractures or massive areas known as fault zones or systems. The San Andreas Fault is such a fault system. It is more than 800 miles (1,278km) long and up to 10 miles (16km) deep. It slices through two-thirds of California. The San Andreas Fault was created by the constant grinding together of the Pacific Ocean plate and North American plate. It took about 10 million years to form.

Nature's Violence

The same plate movement that creates faults can also cause earthquakes. These natural disasters do not always occur in fault zones, but most of them do. That is because the constant grinding, shifting, and crunching of plates causes tremendous pressure to

Earthquakes can cause massive sea waves called tsunamis.

build up. When the pressure becomes too great, massive rocks along the plate boundaries can suddenly snap. This sends out vibrations known as **seismic** waves, and an earthquake is born.

Geologists say that millions of earthquakes happen every year. Most of them are too small for humans to feel, or even for seismic devices to detect. Science journalist Daniel Pendick explains: "If you imagine the Earth as a giant bell, it's ringing with earthquakes every second of the day—from the [subtle] clinks of microquakes to the deafening gong of very occasional but 'great' earthquakes."[7] When such "great" earthquakes do occur, the results can be devastating.

An earthquake in December 2004 caused one of the deadliest natural disasters in history. It was an underwater quake that struck far below the Indian Ocean. It was caused by a collision between the India and Burma plates. The lighter Burma plate abruptly snapped upward, causing the seafloor to burst open. This resulted in a violent explosion. The energy rocketed through the water, triggering a massive sea wave known as a **tsunami**. Hundreds of thousands of people were killed or injured.

Earth appears to be rock solid and stable, but it is not. It is constantly on the move, its gigantic plates adrift on the hot, soft mantle below. Over millions of years, the movement has radically changed the planet. Because Earth is never still, it will continue to evolve and change.

Chapter 3

Earth's Natural Wonders

Throughout history, the same powerful forces that changed Earth's crust have also created natural works of art. From enormous mountain ranges to deep canyons, these wonders can be found in nearly every corner of the planet.

Giant Folds of Land

Earth's mountains are a dramatic example of how plate movement shapes the landscape.

Large mountain ranges were formed over millions of years. These enormous masses of rock are created in different ways. Folded mountains get their start when two continental plates collide. Because these landmasses are about the same weight, one plate cannot be forced beneath the other. Instead, the great pressure of the collision buckles and folds the crust like modeling clay. The folded rock will keep pushing upward until a mountain is formed.

The Himalayas formed as a result of the collision between the Eurasian and Indian continental plates.

Folded mountains resemble massive waves of rock. One of the most spectacular of these mountain ranges is the snowcapped Himalayas. They stretch across six countries on the Asian continent. The Himalayas are the world's highest mountains. They started to form between 40 and 50 million years ago, when the Eurasian and Indian plates collided and kept pushing against each other. The USGS explains: "The pressure of the [colliding] plates could only be relieved by thrusting skyward

. . . and forming the jagged Himalayan peaks."[8] Mount Everest, which is located in the country of Nepal, is part of the Himalayas. Towering at more than 29,000 feet (8,839m) high, it is the tallest continental mountain on Earth.

The Appalachians are known as old fold mountains because they are so ancient. They are the oldest mountains in North America. The Appalachians began forming more than 300 million years ago. They stretch more than 1,500 miles (2,414km), from Quebec, Canada, to central Alabama. The Blue Ridge Mountains and Great Smoky Mountains are part of the Appalachian range.

Fault Blocks and Domes

On the western side of the United States are California's Sierra Nevada Mountains. They are young compared to the Appalachians. They are only about 40 million years old. The Sierra Nevadas are fault-block mountains. They formed at fault lines as plates moved apart from each other. This movement stretched the crust as though it were made of elastic. When it snapped, forces within Earth pushed large blocks of crust upward. As this continued to happen, the mountain range was born.

The Black Hills of South Dakota are known as dome mountains. Unlike folded or fault-block mountains, dome mountains are not formed by crust that snaps or buckles. They are created by hot

The Sierra Nevada mountains in California formed at fault lines when the Earth's tectonic plates moved.

molten material known as **magma**. It comes from inside Earth's mantle, where it is stored in reservoirs known as magma chambers. Magma is lighter than the surrounding rock, so it rises. In areas where dome mountains are found, the thick, flowing substance does not reach the surface. It cools and hardens beneath the ground, forming a mountain's core. This forces heavy rocks out of the crust and up onto the surface. As more magma rises and hardens, it expands the core. That pushes even more rocks upward. Over time, this forms dome-like mountains that resemble giant blisters.

Fire Mountains

Volcanoes are also formed by magma. They are different from dome mountains, however, because the magma does not harden below the ground. Instead, the hot, molten rock escapes through cracks in the crust. It may bubble quietly to the surface, or it may erupt in a violent explosion. Once the magma has reached the crust, it is called lava.

As much as 90 percent of the world's volcanoes are clustered around plate boundaries. That is because volcanoes are created by the same tectonic forces that cause earthquakes. Mount St. Helens in southern Washington State was formed by the sinking, or subduction, of an oceanic plate beneath a

The Mount St. Helens volcano formed with the subduction of an oceanic plate beneath a continental plate.

continental plate. For years it appeared to be a serene, snowcapped mountain. Most people knew that it was a volcano. But because it had been dormant, or quiet, since the 1800s, they were not worried. Then on May 18, 1980, Mount St. Helens erupted in a violent explosion. The blast was more powerful than 10 million tons (9.1 million tonnes) of dynamite. A giant mushroom-shaped cloud of ash rose 15 miles (24km) into the sky. The eruption ripped off one whole side of the volcano. An enormous avalanche of hot ash and lava poured out of the opening. It thundered down the side of the volcano, traveling at more than 200 miles per hour (320kph). The fiery mass destroyed everything in its path, including homes, roads, and entire forests. By the time Mount St. Helens was quiet again, 63 people were dead.

"Gentle Volcanoes"

Not all volcanoes are as violent as Mount St. Helens. For example, the volcanoes in Hawaii are different from those in many other parts of the world. Rob Pacheco, a tour guide in Hawaii, explains: "In other places when a volcano erupts people flee for their lives. In Hawaii we get in our cars and drive down to the lava flow to check it out. In many ways they are gentle volcanoes; they are volcanoes with aloha."[9]

Unlike most volcanoes, those found in Hawaii did not form at plate boundaries. The Hawaiian Is-

Magma oozes gently and slowly from a Hawaiian volcano.

lands are in the middle of the oceanic Pacific plate.
Volcanic areas such as these are known as hot spots.
There is much less gas and pressure in the magma
chambers of hot spots. So magma oozes out of the
ground gently and easily, rather than in a sudden
explosion.

All the islands in the Hawaiian chain were formed
by the slow buildup of volcanic lava. These volcanoes are called shield volcanoes because their wide,
rounded shape resembles a warrior's shield. The

biggest island, Hawaii, is made up of seven volcanoes. Five are on the surface and two are underwater. One of the underwater volcanoes is Mauna Kea. The part aboveground is 13,790 feet (4,203m) high. But when measured from bottom to top, Mauna Kea is more than 32,000 feet (9,754m) high. That makes Mauna Kea the tallest mountain on Earth—even taller than Mount Everest!

Mountain Lying Down

Earth's deep canyons are just as awe-inspiring as mountains and volcanoes. The Grand Canyon, located in Arizona, is considered one of nature's most beautiful creations. It covers 1,904 square miles (4,920 sq km)—more than the state of Rhode Is-

The Grand Canyon was formed by erosion from wind, rain, and the Colorado River.

land. The massive canyon is 217 miles (349km) long, up to 18 miles (29km) wide, and more than a mile (1.6km) deep. Centuries ago, Native American peoples known as the Paiutes gave it their own name: Mountain Lying Down.

The Grand Canyon contains some of the oldest rocks on the planet. The rock that lines its walls tells stories about Earth's history. Each layer of rock represents a different geologic age. The layers at the bottom were formed as many as 2 billion years ago. Geologists believe the canyon was once a towering mountain range. It may have been as high as the Himalayas. Over millions of years, erosion from wind and rain wore the mountains down. Then about 6 million years ago, the Colorado River started to eat away at them. Bit by bit, the river's powerful, rushing waters carved the canyon out of solid rock. Science writer Antony Mason describes the majestic view today: "The winding slit of a canyon creates a dramatic and ever-changing spectacle of light and shadow, [from] the daylight hours that pass between the cool mists of a lingering dawn to the red and orange fireworks of sunset."[10]

The Earth is a mosaic of natural wonders. Snow-capped mountains, fire-breathing volcanoes, and deep gouges carved in the earth by rushing water are all spectacular examples of the power of nature.

Chapter 4

Scientists at Work

Scientists who study Earth work in different ways. Some travel to distant places to examine fault lines, volcanoes, or ridges and trenches on the ocean floor. Others work in laboratories, using powerful microscopes and computers to analyze ancient rocks. Wherever they work, their goal is to learn more about Earth and how it formed.

Rock Science

Geologists have learned a great deal about Earth from studying rocks. The entire planet is made of rock, from the ocean floor to mountain ranges and canyons. According to the USGS, the oldest rock ever found was 4 billion years old. Even though rocks have changed over time, they tell the story of Earth's history.

Geologist Greg Hirth spends much of his time studying rocks. He says that no matter what type they are, all rocks are made of crystals. Studying these crystal structures helps Hirth learn how rocks behave under different conditions. He explains:

"Just the way a solid metal paper clip—when heat or force is applied—can bend, break, or stretch, so, too, can the crystal fabric within rocks."[11]

Hirth performs experiments in which he subjects rocks to the same pressures and temperatures that they experience on Earth. This shows him how rocks behave under various conditions. For example, he can see how much stress it takes to crack a rock, or at what temperature a rock begins to melt. This research helps Hirth and other scientists learn more about earthquakes, including the forces behind them and how deep in the crust they are likely to occur.

All types of rocks are made up of crystals.

Deep Drilling

Geologists gather some of their rock samples by pulling them out of the deep parts of Earth's crust. They may go on research trips for weeks or months. These expeditions take place out in the ocean, because oceanic crust is much thinner than continental crust. Researchers use enormous drills to bore into the seafloor. They want to get as close as possible to the mantle, although such deep drilling is not easy.

In November 2006 a team of scientists drilled deeper than anyone had before. They were part of an expedition called the Integrated Ocean Drilling Program (IODP). It took place in the Pacific Ocean,

Geological drilling allows scientists to gather rock samples and information about the Earth's composition.

where the crust is about 15 million years old. The scientists drilled through nearly a mile (1.4km) of solid rock. After almost six months, they finally reached a magma chamber within the crust. They took samples of a black rock known as gabbros that had originally formed in the mantle. Scientist Neil Banerjee described this sort of exploration: "I would say this is just like a voyage of discovery to the planet Mars, except this is inner space rather than outer space. We're learning about the fundamental dynamics of how our planet works."[12]

A Window into the Earth

Several years before the IODP expedition, a team of scientists made an astounding discovery in the Atlantic Ocean. They found a huge gash the size of a small city on the seafloor. There was no crust over it at all—the mantle was completely exposed. It was found with **sonar** technology. The sonar instruments formed pictures of the area using sound waves. Although the scientists did not understand why the gash was there, they were very excited to find it. They saw it as a window into the inside of Earth.

In March 2007 a team of British scientists returned to the spot to study it further. They used sonar devices to create an image of the ocean floor. Then a car-sized undersea robot named Toby landed on the exposed mantle. The robot drilled into it, gathered samples of the greenish rock, and returned it to the

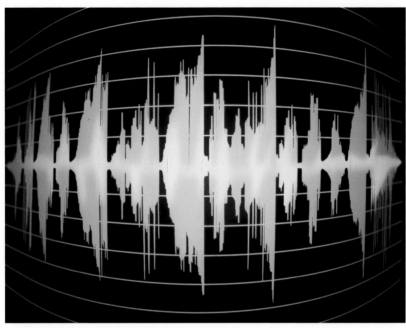

Sonar technology enables scientists to form pictures of the seafloor using sound waves.

ship. Chris MacLeod explains why finding the gash was so important: "This discovery is like an open wound on the surface of the Earth. Was the crust never there? Was it once there but then torn away on huge geological faults? If so, then how and why?"[13] MacLeod hopes that the sample rock will provide answers to those questions. He also believes it will allow scientists to learn more about Earth's mysterious mantle.

Recycled Rock

Scientists also use seismic waves to explore Earth's deep layers. Seismic waves are like sound waves, but they travel through rock instead of air. As the waves move through Earth, computers record them and take pictures.

This sort of technology helped a team of researchers from California make a surprising discovery in 2006. They found a gigantic slab of folded crust close to the planet's core. The slab was more than 125 miles (201km) wide and 370 miles (595km) long. The researchers believe it was once part of the ocean floor. About 50 million years ago, it started to sink when one plate was shoved beneath another. They could tell that the slab was not hard and rigid like normal crust. Instead it was soft, like taffy. Scientists believe this discovery is proof of Earth's ability to recycle itself. As old crust is folded into the planet, it sinks to the bottom of the mantle. That displaces existing mantle rock, forcing some of it upward to form new crust.

Earthquake Studies

Seismic technology also helps scientists learn about earthquakes. In July 2005 researchers used seismic instruments to study a fault zone beneath the Japanese city of Tokyo. Japan is one of the most earthquake-prone countries on the planet. Tokyo is especially at risk because it was built atop the boundaries of three plates: the Eurasian plate, the Philippine Sea plate, and the Pacific plate.

On this mission, scientists used air guns and explosives to force seismic signals deep into the ocean

Seismic technology helps scientists learn about earthquakes and aids development of earthquake warning systems.

floor. They listened for seismic waves to bounce back and then created a computer-generated image. What they discovered was troublesome. A major earthquake-producing fault was closer to the surface than they originally thought. That meant Tokyo is even more at risk for severe earthquakes than scientists had believed. They hope this information will help them determine how strong future quakes will be. Then they can try to develop better warning systems.

"Lava Bombs"

Because Japan is as prone to volcanic eruptions as it is earthquakes, it is an excellent place for scientists to study volcanoes. In April 2006 a team of researchers was studying a large volcano on the seafloor south of Japan—and they got a big surprise.

The researchers were using remote-control devices to guide a robot called Jason. The robot traveled along the seafloor, connected to the research vessel. It was equipped with cameras, as well as a

Lava spews from a volcano on Kilauea, Hawaii.

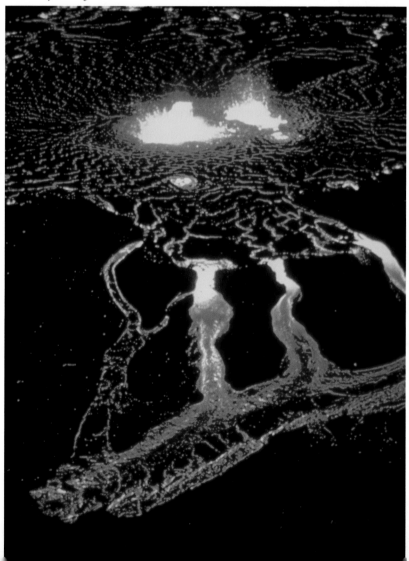

hydrophone that recorded sound. It was studying an area of the volcano that was bubbling quietly. Suddenly the bubbling changed to a violent explosion. Jason's cameras captured images of the volcano spewing huge, billowing clouds of gas, rocks, and red-hot lava up into the water.

One of the researchers, Will Sellers, said that "lava bombs as big as your head" were stuck on Jason when the robot came up to the surface. Bob Elder, a scientist who has participated in 81 research expeditions, describes what the experience was like: "The eruption certainly was the frosting on the cake for the cruise, and one of the coolest, most dramatic things I've seen on the bottom of any ocean."[14]

Whether they examine rocks in laboratories or spend months on ocean research expeditions, scientists are constantly learning about Earth. In the future, as technology gets even more sophisticated, they will continue to gain knowledge. Their goal is to unlock even more of the planet's many mysteries.

Chapter 1: An Ancient Planet

1. Lynn Rosentrater, "Looking at the Sea: The Water Cycle," The Museum of Science (www.mos.org/oceans/planet/cycle.html).
2. W. Jacquelyne Kious and Robert I. Tilling, "This Dynamic Earth: The Story of Plate Tectonics," February 1996. http://pubs.usgs.gov/gip/dynamic/dynamic.pdf.

Chapter 2: Earth on the Move

3. Kirk Maasch, "Continents on the Move," Nova Online, *Cracking the Ice Age*, September 30, 1997. www.pbs.org/wgbh/nova/ice/continents.
4. Quoted in Patrick Hughes, "The Meteorologist Who Started a Revolution," *Pangaea*, April 1994. http://pangaea.org/wegener.htm.
5. Kious and Tilling, "This Dynamic Earth."
6. Joseph B. Verrengia, "Earthquakes Still Mapmaking After 300 Million Years," SouthCoastToday, January 9, 2005. www.southcoasttoday.com/daily/01-05/01-09-05/b04pe091.htm.
7. Daniel Pendick, "Earth: All Stressed Out," PBS *Savage Earth*, July 1998. www.pbs.org/wnet/savageearth/earthquakes/index.html.

Chapter 3: Earth's Natural Wonders

8. Kious and Tilling, "This Dynamic Earth."
9. Rob Pacheco, "A Hot Spot of Aloha," Hawaii Forest and Trail. www.hawaii-forest.com/essays/9712.html.

10. Antony Mason, *Strange Worlds, Fantastic Places*. London: Reader's Digest, 1997, p. 24.

Chapter 4: Scientists at Work

11. Greg Hirth, "Peering into the Crystal Fabric of Rocks," Woods Hole Oceanographic Institution Deep Ocean Exploration Institute, June 22, 2004. www.whoi.edu/insti tutes/doei/viewArticle.do?id=2494.
12. Quoted in Michael Graczyk, "Experts Hope Rocks Unravel Earth's Secrets," *USA Today*, June 18, 2006. www.usa today.com/tech/science/discoveries/2006-06-18-rocks-earth_x.htm.
13. Quoted in "Earth's Crust Missing in Mid-Atlantic," Science Daily, March 2, 2007. www.sciencedaily.com/re leases/2007/03/070301103112.htm.
14. Quoted in Amy E. Nevala, "Jason Versus the Volcano," Woods Hole Oceanographic Institution Deep Ocean Exploration Institute, August 4, 2006. www.whoi.edu/in stitutes/doei/viewArticle.do?id=14507.

Glossary

continental: Relating to Earth's continents.

continental drift: A theory developed by Alfred Wegener that the planet's continents were once joined and then separated and drifted apart.

core: The solid iron center of Earth (inner core) and the molten layer that surrounds it (outer core).

crust: Earth's rocky top layer.

faults: Cracks in Earth's crust that result from plate movement.

geologists: Scientists who specialize in studying Earth and rock formations.

magma: Molten rock beneath the Earth's surface.

mantle: The layer that surrounds Earth's outer core.

molten: Melted.

nebula: A huge space cloud made up of gas and dust.

oceanic: Relating to Earth's oceans.

ozone layer: The protective layer of Earth's atmosphere that helps screen out the Sun's harmful ultraviolet rays.

seismic: Related to vibrations in the Earth.

sonar: A type of technology that uses sound waves to create pictures of underwater objects.

subduction: The sinking of a heavier tectonic plate beneath a lighter one.

tsunami: A massive sea wave triggered by violent disturbances in Earth, such as earthquakes.

For Further Exploration

Books

Paula Manzanero, *Scholastic Atlas of Earth*. New York: Scholastic, 2005. This book unlocks the mysteries of the planet by discussing Earth's tectonic plates, mountains and volcanoes, fossils, minerals and gems, and other natural wonders.

Mary Varilla, *Scholastic Atlas of Oceans*. New York: Scholastic, 2004. Discusses where Earth's oceans are, how they formed, what causes waves, how coastlines were created, and the kinds of creatures that live in the ocean.

Volcanoes & Earthquakes. New York: Dorling Kindersley Children, 2004. A beautifully illustrated book that helps young readers understand the science behind these natural disasters.

Claire Watts and Trevor Day, *Natural Disasters*. New York: Dorling Kindersley, 2006. Explains the causes and impacts of hurricanes, tsunamis, and other deadly natural disasters.

Magazine Articles

David Hill, "Slow Slide," *Touchdown*, August 2005, pp. 230–32. This is a fascinating article about avalanches that occur deep beneath Earth's surface.

Lisa P. Hill, "Rocks and Geology," *Science Weekly*, April 11, 2006, pp. C-1+. Hill discusses Earth's different layers and how scientists study rocks to better understand the planet's history.

Chris Jozefowicz, "Ripple Effect," *Current Science*, December 16, 2005, pp. 10+. This article explains what scientists have learned about the underwater earthquake that led to the deadly Southeast Asian tsunami of December 2004.

Internet Article

Robert Roy Britt, "101 Amazing Earth Facts," Space.com, July 22, 2003. www.space.com/scienceastronomy/101 _earth_facts_030722-1.html. Britt answers all kinds of questions about Earth and its natural wonders.

Web Sites

Extreme Science (www.extremescience.com). This site includes a wealth of information about Earth, its oceans, plate tectonics, natural disasters such as tsunamis and earthquakes, and the mysteries of the planet's vast oceans.

How Stuff Works (http://science.howstuffworks.com). This site includes several well-written articles on Earth-related topics

NASA For Kids Only: Earth Science Enterprise (http:// kids.earth.nasa.gov). An excellent resource for young people, this site includes facts about Earth's land, water, atmosphere, and natural hazards. It also explains how NASA studies Earth.

USGS Earthquakes for Kids (http://earthquake.usgs.gov/ learning/kids.php). Designed to help young people have fun while they gain a better understanding of earthquakes, this site includes pictures of earthquakes, puzzles and games, "Cool Earthquake Facts," frequently asked questions, and an "Ask a Geologist" forum.

Index

Picture Credits

Cover photo: photos.com
© Gary Braasch/CORBIS, 25
© Ric Ergenbright/CORBIS, 22
© Sally A. Morgan/CORBIS, 24
Warren Bolster/Photographer's Choice/Getty Images, 19
DEA picture Library/Getty Images, 31
Tommy Flyn/Photographer's Choice/Getty Images, 34
Lui Jin/AFP/Getty Images, 32
NASA/Getty Images, 5
Michael Urban/AFP/Getty Images, 36
JLM Visuals, 37
National Aeronautics and Space Administration, 11
National Oceanic and Atomospheric Administration, 8
Macmillan Reference Library, 18
Christian Darkin/Photo Researcher's, Inc., 14
Gary Hincks/Photo researcher's, Inc., 6, 16, 17
Planetary Visions, Ltd., Photo Researcher's, Inc., 9
Courtesy of the National Park Service, 27
Courtesy of the U.S. Geological Survey, 28

Peggy J. Parks holds a bachelor of science degree from Aquinas College in Grand Rapids, Michigan, where she graduated magna cum laude. She is a freelance author who has written more than 60 nonfiction books for children and young adults. Parks lives in Muskegon, Michigan, a town that she says inspires her writing because of its location on the shores of Lake Michigan.